NATURE FILES
ANIMAL FAMILIES

NATURE FILES – ANIMAL FAMILIES
was produced by

David West ⚇ Children's Books
7 Princeton Court
55 Felsham Road
London SW15 1AZ

Designer: Julie Joubinaux
Editor: Gail Bushnell
Picture Research: Carlotta Cooper

First published in Great Britain by Heinemann
Library, Halley Court, Jordan Hill, Oxford
OX2 8EJ, part of Harcourt Education.
Heinemann is a registered trademark
of Harcourt Education Ltd.

07 06 05 04 03
10 9 8 7 6 5 4 3 2 1

ISBN 0 431 18243 4 (HB)
ISBN 0 431 18250 7 (PB)

Printed and bound in Italy

PHOTO CREDITS :
Abbreviations: t-top, m-middle, b-bottom, r-right,
l-left, c-centre.

Front cover - all Corbis Images. 3 & 13b, 23t (David
Kjaer), 4–5, 9t, 29b (John Cancalosi), 5t, 26–27t, 29
(Pete Oxford), 6l, 21t (Jeff Foott), 6r, 8bl, 18b, 24t,
25bl (Anup Shah), 7tl (G & H. Denzau), 7b (Duncan
McEwan), 8t, 15m (Tom Vezo), 11m (Sharon Heald)
11b (Doug Allan), 12b (Herman Brehm), 13tl (Yuri
Shibnev), 13tr (Nick Gordon), 15b (Neil Lucas), 17b
22 (Staffan Widstrand), 18t, 19t (John Downer), 18l
(David Welling), 19b (Richard Brock), 20 (Ron
O'Connor), 21bl (Neil Bromhall), 23m (Bengt
Lundberg), 25br (Louis Gagnon), 26–27b (Jurgen
Freund), 27t (Thomas D. Mangelsen), 27b
(Premaphotos), 28–29 (Tony Heald) - naturepl.com.
4t (M & C. Denis-Huot), 7t (Bruno Cavignaux), 14
(Jean-Claude Teyssier), 20–21 (Lynn Rogers), 26 (J.P.
Delobelle), 28br (Fred Bruemmer) - Still Pictures. 5b,
8br, 16 both, 17tl & tr, 21br, 23b, 28bl - Corbis
Images. 9b (Tim Shepherd), 10r (Rudie Kuiter), 12t
(Mark Deebie & Victoria Stone), 24b (Daniel Cox) -
Oxford Scientific Films. 10l (Scott Tuason), 11t (Alex
Haas), 15t (Paul Harcourt), 22–23 (Chris Parks) -
Image Quest 3D.

Every effort has been made to contact copyright
holders of any material reproduced in this book. Any
omissions will be rectified in subsequent printings if
notice is given to the publishers.

*An explanation of difficult words can be
found in the glossary on page 31.*

NATURE FILES

ANIMAL FAMILIES

Anita Ganeri

Heinemann LIBRARY

CONTENTS

Lions live in family groups called prides. A pride is mostly made up of related females and their young, with one or two adult males. The pride co-operates in hunting prey that would be too large for a single lion to tackle.

Many birds work in pairs to care for their young. Once the chicks hatch, they are always hungry and feeding them is hard work. Sharing these duties is the only way of making sure the chicks, and their parents, get enough to eat.

INTRODUCTION

From huge flocks of flamingoes and shoals of fish, to small troops of apes, many animals live in some sort of family group. Living in a family has many advantages. Animals can produce and raise their young in safety. Many also work together to find food and defend the group against enemies. Some families are highly organised, with a definite 'pecking order'. Others are loose collections of animals from the same species.

In many families, the mother animal raises the young. Female mammals, such as ring-tailed lemurs, feed their young on milk and look after them until they can fend for themselves. The young lemurs often ride along on their mother's back.

Many small fish live in vast shoals. This is much safer than living on their own. Predators find it difficult to pick out and catch an individual from among the crowd.

In nature, there are many types of family. The simplest is made up of parents and their young. But other relatives, such as cousins, aunts, uncles and grandparents may also be part of the family.

WHY HAVE FAMILIES?

For animals to survive, they must produce young who will continue their species. One advantage of living in a family is that it is easier for animals to feed and care for their young. This gives the young a better chance of survival.

Amazing FACT

The animals that help and care for their young for the longest time are human beings. Parents look after their children for many years. Humans also have the longest-lasting family ties. Unlike other animals, members of a human family generally keep in touch with each other throughout their lives.

Many fish hardly care for their young at all. Instead, they put all their energy into mass production. By producing thousands of eggs, they hope that some will survive.

Chimpanzees live in close-knit family groups. The bonds between mothers and their babies are very strong, and often last until the young grow into adults at about 13–15 years old.

Kingfisher parents share the task of collecting food for their hungry chicks. Between them they may have to catch up to 100 fish each day.

Human families are the closest of all.

PARENTAL CARE

The amount of care animals give to their young varies greatly from species to species. Many types of fish, insects and other invertebrates simply lay their eggs, then leave the young to hatch and fend for themselves. Other animals, such as mammals, feed, care for and protect their offspring for many years. Some young animals are looked after by both parents; others by their mother or father alone.

Most insects are not caring parents. Having laid their eggs, they leave them to hatch. Unusually, parent bugs shelter their newly-hatched babies with their bodies to protect them from predators.

MOTHERS AND BABIES

For many animals, it is the mother who cares for the young, usually on her own. The young stay close to their mother, who feeds them and watches over them.

MOTHERLY LOVE

Female mammals produce milk for their young to suckle, so babies are usually looked after by their mothers. Young orang-utans are weaned at about three years old, but stay with their mothers until they are about seven years old.

To beg for food, a seagull chick pecks at a red spot on the underneath of its mother's beak. She then regurgitates food for it.

IMPRINTING

A newly-hatched cygnet becomes attached to the first thing it sees, usually its mother. It follows her wherever she goes and copies her. This is called imprinting. In this way, the young bird recognises its parent and safety. Imprinting can go wrong. If the first thing a young bird sees is a another animal, it will attach to it.

Cygnets swim safely with their mother.

A baby orang-utan suckling. The tiny baby clings to its mother as she moves around to look for food.

Young scorpions ride on their mother's back, out of the reach of enemies, until they are either too large for her to carry around or old enough to take care of themselves.

LOOKING AFTER BABY

Mother animals also protect their young from harm. Some animals carry their young about to keep them safe. A desert scorpion's eggs hatch into miniature versions of the adults. They immediately climb on to their mother's back, and cling on tightly with their tiny pincers and legs. If they fall off, their mother waits for them to climb back on again.

Amazing FACT

Unusually for an insect, the female earwig is a caring mother. She digs a hole in the ground and lays her eggs in it. For safety, she sits over them, cleaning and turning them regularly to prevent infection. She continues to guard the baby earwigs for a week or two after they hatch.

An earwig mother with her eggs.

9

Some young animals are raised and looked after by their fathers, although this is not very common. This allows the females to go off to feed or to mate again.

CARING FOR THE EGGS

It is usually the female who carries the eggs. But, during mating, a female seahorse squirts hundreds of eggs into a pouch on the male's belly where they are fertilised and nourished. About a month later, they hatch into tiny babies which shoot out of their father's pouch and into the sea.

A male cardinalfish incubates his eggs in his mouth for a week. During this time he goes without food. When the young fish hatch, he spits them out into the water.

Seahorses do not have nests, so the male's pouch provides a safe place for the eggs to develop.

A female midwife toad lays her eggs, then the male looks after them. He carries them around on his back until they are ready to hatch. Then he lowers his back into water so that the tadpoles can swim out.

DOTING FATHERS

For many male birds, attracting a mate is more important than looking after eggs or young. However, some male birds are doting fathers. Among ostriches, the job of caring for the eggs is often left to the male. Several females lay eggs in his nest. He sits on them to incubate them and protect them from predators.

Among water birds called jacanas, it is the males who build the nests, incubate the eggs and look after the young. If danger threatens, the male carries his chicks to safety under his wings.

Male emperor penguins with their eggs.

Amazing FACT

A female emperor penguin lays her egg in the middle of the freezing Antarctic winter. Then she goes off to sea to feed until the spring. The male balances the egg on his feet, tucked under a fold of warm skin. Then he stands for months on end, not moving or eating, until the chick hatches out.

11

TWO-PARENT FAMILY

Many animal parents share the care of their young. They work as a team to protect their offspring from danger and to find food.

PAIRING FOR LIFE

Some animals only pair up for breeding. Then they go their separate ways. Swans, though, have a strong bond and often pair for life. They share their parental duties equally, building their nest and caring for their young together.

Cichlid fish share the care of their young. They build their nest together, and guard the eggs and young fish. Some carry their eggs and young in their mouths to protect them from predators.

Within a large flock of swans, there are several family groups of parent birds and their cygnets. Both parents work hard to keep the cygnets safe.

Both marmoset parents carry the babies on their backs as they search for food among the trees.

Golden eagles build huge nests of twigs and branches over 4 metres deep, high up in the trees. The same nest may be used, year after year, for over 40 years.

SHARING CARE

A two-parent family gives young animals a better chance of survival. With both a mother and father to look after them, the young are likely to be well fed and well protected. For many birds, including golden eagles, both parents take turns to guard their nests and fetch food for their chicks.

GOOD DADS

A titi monkey family is made up of a male, female and several offspring. The father plays a large part in caring for the young. A baby monkey rides around on its father's back until it can easily keep up with the adults on its own.

Amazing FACT
Some animals rely on foster parents to raise their young. A female European cuckoo lays her egg in another bird's nest. When the cuckoo chick hatches, it pushes the other chicks out of the nest and takes all their food for itself.

A cuckoo chick imposter.

Female   Male

Young

Titi family

13

EXTENDED FAMILIES

Some animals live in larger groups and communities. These groups are often highly organised, with any work shared out among the various members of the family.

SOCIAL INSECTS

Social insects, including bees, wasps and ants, live in huge colonies, many thousands strong. Within the colony, each insect has its own job to do. The queen lays the eggs and other members of the colony find food, build and guard the nest and care for the young.

Among social insects, all the insects work together for the good of the colony. In a honeybee colony, worker bees like these build and repair the honeycomb, and forage for food.

SOCIAL UNITS OF A BABOON TROOP

This diagram shows the organisation of a troop of Hamadryas baboons in Ethiopia. They live in highly structured societies. A harem, or family, is made up of a dominant male with several females and their young. Several harems form a 'clan' of 10–20 baboons, which forage and sleep as a group. For safety, clans hunt for food together in a 'band' of about 70 animals. Bands also form a loose group called a 'troop' of about 200 baboons.

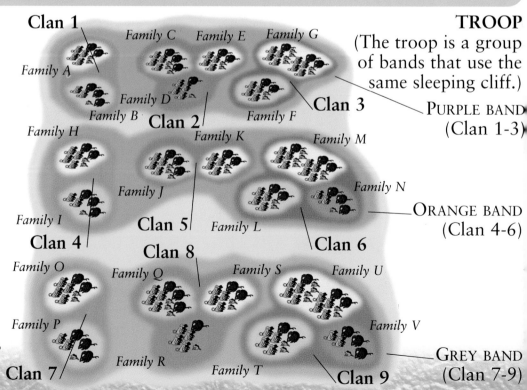

TROOP
(The troop is a group of bands that use the same sleeping cliff.)

PURPLE BAND
(Clan 1-3)

ORANGE BAND
(Clan 4-6)

GREY BAND
(Clan 7-9)

Clan 1, Family A, Family C, Family E, Family G, Family B, Family D, Clan 2, Family F, Clan 3, Family H, Family K, Family M, Family J, Family N, Family I, Clan 5, Family L, Clan 6, Clan 4, Clan 8, Family O, Family Q, Family S, Family U, Family P, Family V, Family R, Family T, Clan 9, Clan 7

In an ant colony, all the eggs are laid by one queen. Each year, a group of males leave the nest with the queen and mate with her. Afterwards the males die.

HUGE HAREMS

A harem is a group made up of a single male and many females. Some harems stay together all year round. However, red deer, sea lions and walruses form harems for the breeding season only. For the remainder of the year, the males live apart from the females and their offspring.

A male fur seal with females.

A walrus herd may contain up to 1000 animals. Within a herd this size, there are many harems.

Living among a large group of its own species is an excellent survival tactic for an animal. On its own, a single animal is an easy target for predators. Surrounded by others, it is much trickier to catch.

FLOCKS AND HERDS

Many birds and mammals live in large flocks or herds. Herds of zebras graze on the open plains of Africa. A solitary animal would be easy for lions or wild dogs to pick off. It is much safer being part of a group.

A herd of zebras may be several hundred strong. While the rest of the herd grazes, several zebras keep a look out for danger. If an enemy approaches, they sound the alarm.

Amazing FACT

In the 19th century, huge herds of springbok used to migrate across the plains of southern Africa in search of water and food. One herd was estimated to cover more than 5000 square kilometres and to contain over 10 million animals. Another herd took three days to pass. Herds now number just 1500 animals.

Most types of penguins are highly social birds. They breed in large colonies, called rookeries.

Springbok herds are now quite small.

Larger fish, such as tuna, also form shoals as protection against sailfish and dolphin predators. The tuna themselves prey on shoals of smaller fish.

SHOALING FISH

Many small fish live in vast groups, called shoals, many thousands strong. This protects them against predators. By clustering closely together, individual fish are less likely to be detected than if they were scattered about. The size of the shoal, and the way it moves and changes shape, confuse predators, making it tricky for them to focus on a particular fish.

MUSK OXEN

Musk oxen live in herds of about 15–20 animals. To defend themselves and their calves from wolves, the adult musk oxen form a tight circle, with the calves inside. For extra protection, they lower their heads and present a wall of horns to their attackers. Every so often, a male darts out of the group and launches a surprise attack.

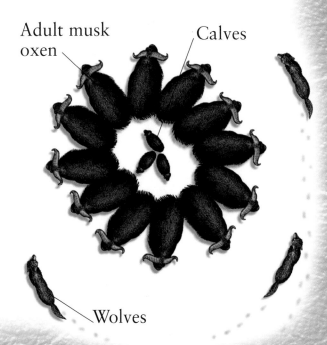

Adult musk oxen

Calves

Wolves

Musk oxen protecting their calves.

The bonds between some animals and their offspring are very strong. Many animal parents go to great lengths to care for their young. They clean them, feed them, carry them from place to place, and keep them safe from danger.

STRONG BONDS

As soon as a baby mammal is born, its mother licks it all over. Not only does this clean the baby but it also helps its mother to recognise its own particular smell. Monkeys and apes continue to groom their offspring as they grow up.

A mother cat carrying a kitten by the scruff of its neck. If her den is disturbed, she carries her kittens, one by one, to a new, safer location.

A plover protecting her eggs.

Amazing FACT

A female plover lays her eggs among the pebbles on a beach. If a predator approaches, she distracts it by running away, dragging one of her wings as if it is broken. Thinking her an easy target, the predator follows. Once away from her nest, she flies off.

Every day, a mother baboon examines her baby's coat and picks off any dirt or ticks. This not only keeps its fur clean but strengthens the bond between mother and baby.

PROTECTING BABY

Faced with danger, some animal parents respond by carrying their babies away to safety. Many mammals, including cats and dogs, pick up their babies by the scruff of their necks and carry them in their mouths. To make it easier to carry, the baby instinctively goes limp, stays very quiet and still, and does not struggle.

A female shrew takes her babies with her when she goes out to feed. The young shrews follow in a line, holding the tail of the one in front.

A young giant anteater may ride on its mother's back for up to a year. The colour of its fur matches its mother exactly, making it hard to see.

TEAMWORK

In some families, animals help to look after their relations and co-operate in finding food. This gives the members of the family a better chance of surviving.

BABY-SITTING

Some animals look after young that are not their own offspring. A young African elephant, for example, is cared for by a group of its close relations. If its mother dies, one of its 'aunts' adopts it as her own. African hunting dogs live in large packs, and raise all their pack's pups together.

A PRIDE OF LIONS

Most cats are solitary but lions are social animals. The members of a pride or group hunt together, share out prey and even help to raise each other's cubs. The pride is largely made up of female cousins. They will suckle cubs that are not their own, increasing the cubs' chances of survival.

By working as a team, wolves hunt large prey, such as a moose or caribou, which they could not tackle on their own.

A female African hunting dog will suckle any pups that are hungry. Later, the adults will bring back meat for all the pups to share.

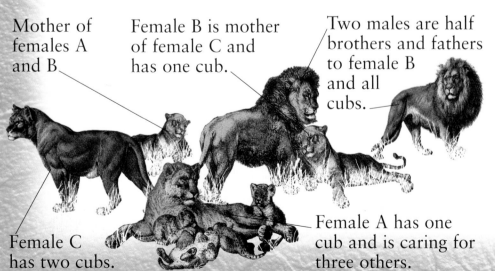

Mother of females A and B.

Female B is mother of female C and has one cub.

Two males are half brothers and fathers to female B and all cubs.

Female C has two cubs.

Female A has one cub and is caring for three others.

HUNTING TOGETHER

Working together to find food is a very efficient way of hunting. A pack of eight to twelve wolves sets out in single file in search of prey. When the wolves spot a moose, for example, they stand very still, then suddenly rush towards it. As soon as the moose starts to run, the wolves attack.

Killer whales band together to attack sea lions.

Amazing FACT

Naked mole rats live in large, underground colonies of up to 80 animals. Each mole rat has its own job to do. One female has all the babies. The other members of the colony care for her offspring, dig tunnels, forage for food and defend the nest against predators.

Naked mole rats.

The members of a meerkat pack all help to look out for danger. If a predator threatens, they will bunch together to drive it off.

Squabbles and disputes can break out among the members of an animal family. These may be arguments over food, mates and territories, or fights to become the leader.

FIGHTING OFF RIVALS

During the breeding season, competition for mates is fierce. Males often use threatening gestures or sounds to warn off rivals. If these do not work, a real fight may break out. Fighting is risky and animals avoid it if they can.

When two male stag beetles fight, each tries to use its horns to get a grip on the other. The winner lifts his rival into the air and throws him on to the ground.

APES BEHAVING BADLY

Gorillas live in family groups of up to 30 animals. Usually, a dominant adult male or silverback, like the one above, is in charge.

Among family groups of apes, there is a definite social order. In chimpanzee troops, rival males threaten each other with dramatic displays as they jostle for position. Males shake tree branches, beat their chests and slap the ground to show who is in charge.

1 Tree shaking

2 Charging and beating chest

3 Slapping the ground

PECKING ORDER

In many animal families, there is a definite pecking order. Some animals are senior and have first choice of food, mates and places to nest and sleep. Some animals are junior and have to work their way up the social order. This system helps to avoid fights because each individual animal knows its place.

Prairie dogs 'kissing'.

Amazing FACT

Prairie dogs live in huge colonies. Sentries guard the burrows and sound the alarm if an intruder is spotted. When two prairie dogs meet, they rub noses to see if they know each other. If they do, they start grooming. If not, the stranger is driven away.

In a flock of swans, squabbles over food are quickly sorted out. A strict hierarchy operates, with family groups having more rights than single swans or pairs without cygnets.

Male antelopes, such as springbok, use their horns or antlers to fight off rivals. They lock horns and charge, often for hours, until one is defeated.

As they grow up, young animals learn by watching and copying their parents, and by playing with each other. They are also born with built-in knowledge which they do not need to learn, called instinct.

PLAY FIGHTING

Many baby mammals learn about the world through play. Playing at climbing, hunting and fighting helps them to develop the skills they will need in their adult lives. They use play-signals, such as special faces or postures, to show their parents that they are just playing.

In play-fights with their brothers and sisters, young cheetahs develop the skills they will need for chasing and hunting prey when they grow up. They also practise pinning prey down, by pouncing on the end of their mother's tail.

These Alaskan brown bear cubs are following their mother as she hunts for fish. By watching her and copying her actions, they will learn to catch fish for themselves.

Amazing FACT

A young animal's cute appearance is vital to its well-being and survival. For example, a baby orang-utan's big eyes, small size and soft fur all send out a specific message. They tell the adults in its family group that it is a baby and that it needs special looking after.

PLAYING FOR REAL

Play fighting

Learning to hunt
small insects

Learning to stalk
a bird

For the first few weeks of its life, a baby squirrel monkey rides on its mother's back. Then it begins to explore and play. It learns how to catch insects to eat, stalk birds, find water and move safely through the trees.

LEARNING TO FLY

Young birds are born with a great deal of instinctive, or built-in, knowledge. They automatically know how to do certain things, such as build their nests and migrate. Young birds instinctively know how to fly, when the time is right, though, they may need a bit of practice.

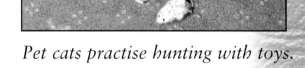

Pet cats practise hunting with toys.

Eagle chicks practise their flight movements by standing on the edge of their nests and flapping their wings.

A baby orang-utan looks cute.

25

At certain times, some animals form enormous groups or swarms. These are not for breeding and are not strictly families. Swarming helps animals to stay safe as they migrate and is a highly effective strategy for hunting.

MIGRATING BIRDS

In preparation for their annual migration, birds form large flocks, many hundreds or thousands strong. Many migrate over long distances and it is much safer for them to travel together than on their own. The birds fly in formation, taking it in turns to lead.

Each year, millions of red crabs emerge from their forest burrows on Christmas Island and migrate across the island to the sea. They feed and then return to the forest.

Flamingoes migrate as part of a large group. This means that, even if some birds are lost on the way, a large number will reach their destination.

In September, swarms of monarch butterflies migrate to Mexico and California for the winter. One swarm was estimated to have over 14 million butterflies.

PLAGUES OF LOCUSTS

On its own, a desert locust is harmless. But at times of food shortages or overcrowding, huge numbers of locusts gather together in massive swarms. They fly over fields, devastating farmers' crops with their huge appetites. In a single day, a swarm of 50 million locusts can eat enough to feed 500 people for a year.

The largest locust swarms may contain 50,000 million insects and cover an area of 1000 square kilometres.

Army ants march in big swarms.

Amazing FACT

Enormous groups of army ants march through the rainforests of Central and South America. An army may stretch for up to 100 metres and contain 600,000 ants. It may take several hours to march past. Any insects, lizards or spiders in its path are eaten.

27

Some animals prefer to live on their own, only meeting up during the breeding season. After mating, one of the parents raises the young. The other parent spends the rest of the year living and hunting alone.

SOLITARY HUNTERS

Many mammals, such as bears and tigers, are solitary hunters. Male and female tigers wander over their own individual home ranges or territories, where they stalk their prey. Tiger cubs stay with their mothers until they are about two years old. Then they find their own ranges.

Polar bears hunt alone, occasionally meeting at a rich food source, such as a whale carcass.

Male tigers live alone and are not involved in raising their cubs.

To advertise his whereabouts to a mate, male sloths mark the branches with a strong-smelling scent.

LIVING ALONE

Sloths live in the rainforests of Central and South America. They are extremely solitary animals, spending up to 18 hours each day asleep. Adults only meet up to breed. A baby sloth is carried by its mother for six to nine months as she hangs upside-down in the trees. The baby has very strong, hook-shaped claws to cling to its mother.

Apart from meeting up to mate, giant pandas are mostly solitary animals. They defend their own forest territory, marking the borders with scent to keep out any intruders.

Batty colony

• The world's largest colony of bats is found in several caves in Texas, USA. The 20 million Mexican free-tailed bats gather to breed.

Identical quads

• Most mammals have babies which look different and are of different sexes. The nine-banded armadillo gives birth to litters of quads. All four babies always look identical and are the same sex.

Caring crocodiles

• People used to think that crocodiles ate their young, but they are caring parents. The female picks up her newborn babies in her mouth and carries them to the water for their first swim.

Powerful pack

• In the 19th century, packs of African wild dogs had 500 animals.

Swarming krill

• Krill are small, shrimp-like creatures which form enormous swarms. The largest swarm on record was thought to weigh about 10 million tonnes.

Crabby mother

• The only type of crab known to look after its young when they hatch is the bromeliad crab from Jamaica. The female lays her eggs in a pool of water which has formed in bromeliad leaves. When the young crabs hatch, she fetches them food to eat and chases off any predators.

Large litter

• In 1972, a common tenrec in a zoo in the Netherlands gave birth to 31 babies in a single litter. This is the largest litter ever for any wild mammal. The normal litter size for a common tenrec is between 10 and 12 babies.

GLOSSARY

dominant
An animal that is in charge.

fertilised
When a female animal's eggs are mixed with a male's sperm so that they grow into babies.

hierarchy
A family or social group in which each animal knows its place.

incubate
How animals keep their eggs warm. Birds sit on them and some fish hold them inside their mouths.

invertebrates
Animals without a backbone or skeleton inside their bodies.

mammals
Animals, such as humans, that feed or suckle their young on milk.

migrate
When animals, such as birds, make long journeys between their feeding and breeding grounds.

predators
Animals that hunt and kill other animals, called prey, for food.

regurgitate
Sick or spit up food.

shoal
A very large group of fish.

solitary
An animal that lives and forages for food on its own.

species
A group of living things that are grouped together because they have similar features.

territory
An area or patch of land which provides animals with food and a safe place to live. Animals defend their territories fiercely.

weaned
When a baby animal stops drinking its mother's milk and starts eating solid food instead.